Disgusting Body Facts

Ooze and Goo

Angela Royston

Raintree

www.raintreepublishers.co.uk
Visit our website to find out more information about Raintree books.

To order:
☎ Phone +44
🖨 Fax +44 (0)
💻 Visit www.

©Raintree is an imprint of Capstone Global Library Limited, a company incorporated in England and Wales having its registered office at 7 Pilgrim Street, London, EC4V 6LB – Registered company number: 6695582

"Raintree" is a registered trademark of Pearson Education Limited, under licence to Capstone Global Library Limited

Text © Capstone Global Library Limited 2010
First published in hardback in 2010
The moral rights of the proprietor have been asserted.

Edited by Nancy Dickmann, Sian Smith, and Rebecca Rissman
Designed by Joanna Hinton Malivoire
Original illustrations ©Capstone Global Library 2010
Original illustrations by Christian Slade
Picture research by Tracy Cummins and Tracey Engel
Originated by Capstone Global Library Ltd
Printed and bound in China by Leo Paper Products Ltd

ISBN 978 1 4062 1308 9 (hardback)
14 13 12 11 10
10 9 8 7 6 5 4 3 2 1

British Library Cataloguing in Publication Data
Royston, Angela.
  Ooze and goo. -- (Disgusting body facts)
  1. Body fluids--Juvenile literature. 2. Suppuration--Juvenile literature. 3. Secretion--Juvenile literature.
  I. Title II. Series
  612.4-dc22

Acknowledgements
We would like to thank the following for permission to reproduce photographs:
Alamy pp. **6** (©David Crausby), **22** (©Medical-on-Line); Getty Images pp. **13** (©The Image Bank/David Trood), **26** (©Seymour Hewitt), **27** (©Stone/Andy Roberts); istockphoto p. **29** (©Holly Sisson); Photo Researchers, Inc. pp. **11 top** (©Scimat), **17** (©Dr P. Marazzi), **21** (©Edward Kinsman); Photolibrary p. **25** (©Blend Images); Phototake p. **15** (©Pulse Picture Library/CMP Images); Shutterstock pp. **9** (©Graca Victoria) **11 bottom** (©Oberon); Visuals Unlimited, Inc. p. **19** (©Ralph Hutchings).

Cover photograph of a woman's tongue dripping saliva reproduced with permission of Getty Images (©David Trood).

Some words are shown in bold, **like this**. You can find out what they mean by looking in the glossary.

Contents

Slimy insides

The inside of your body is slimy and slippery. A liquid called **mucus** lines many tubes in your body. Sometimes mucus leaks out as snot and spit.

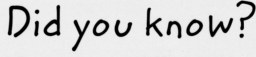

Did you know?

Mucus is not the only thing that leaks from your body. Other things include **ear wax**, blood, and **pus**.

snot

ear wax

spit

pus

5

Snot

Snot is **mucus** in your nose. Snot helps to trap dirt and **germs** that you breathe in. Germs can make you ill. When you have a cold, your nose makes lots of extra mucus. The mucus washes out some of the germs.

bogie

Did you know?

A bogie is dried snot in your nose. Some people pick their noses to remove a bogie! Other people just blow their noses.

7

Coughing up mucus

The tubes that join your mouth and nose to your **lungs** are lined with **mucus**, too. When you are ill, the mucus becomes thick and sticky. Then you cough to clear the tubes.

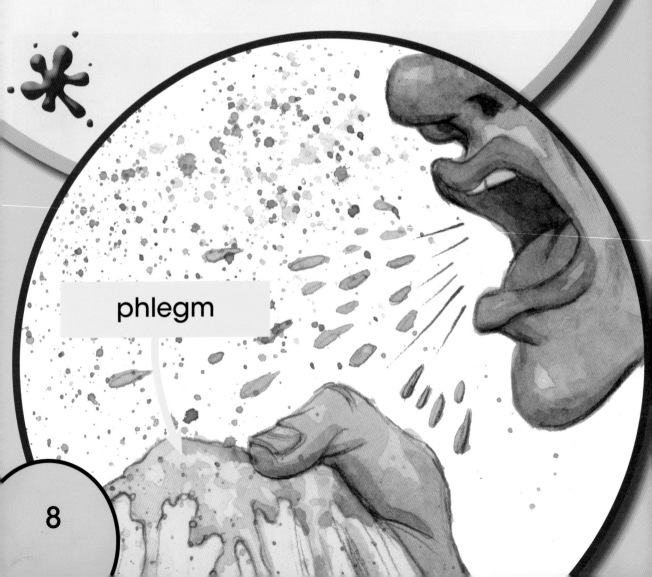

phlegm

8

When you cough, the mucus comes into your mouth. It is called **phlegm** [say "flem"]. Mucus contains **germs**, so never touch someone else's snot or phlegm.

Why is phlegm sometimes green?

When you are ill your **phlegm** might be yellow or green. Your body makes chemicals to kill **germs** when you are ill. The iron in the chemicals turns your phlegm green.

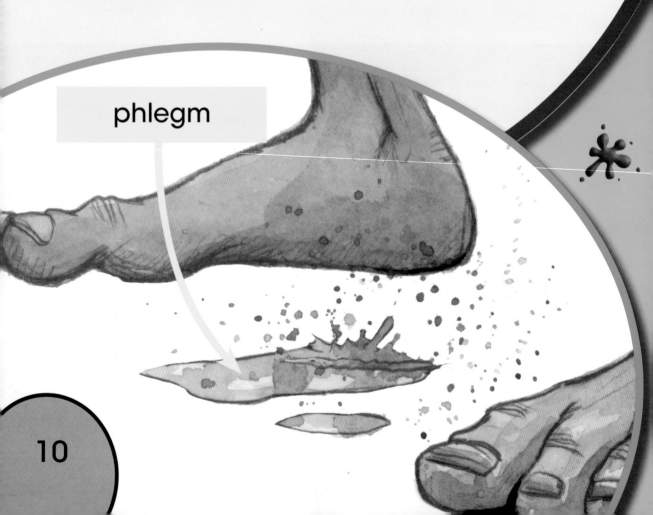

phlegm

microscope

These are germs seen through a microscope.

Did you know?

Germs are too small to see without a microscope. It could take a million of them to cover the head of a pin.

Saliva and spit

Your mouth makes **saliva**, or spit, all the time. When you are asleep, saliva sometimes dribbles out of your mouth. It wets your pillow!

Did you know?

Some people spit when they speak. As they talk, a shower of spit sprays into the air!

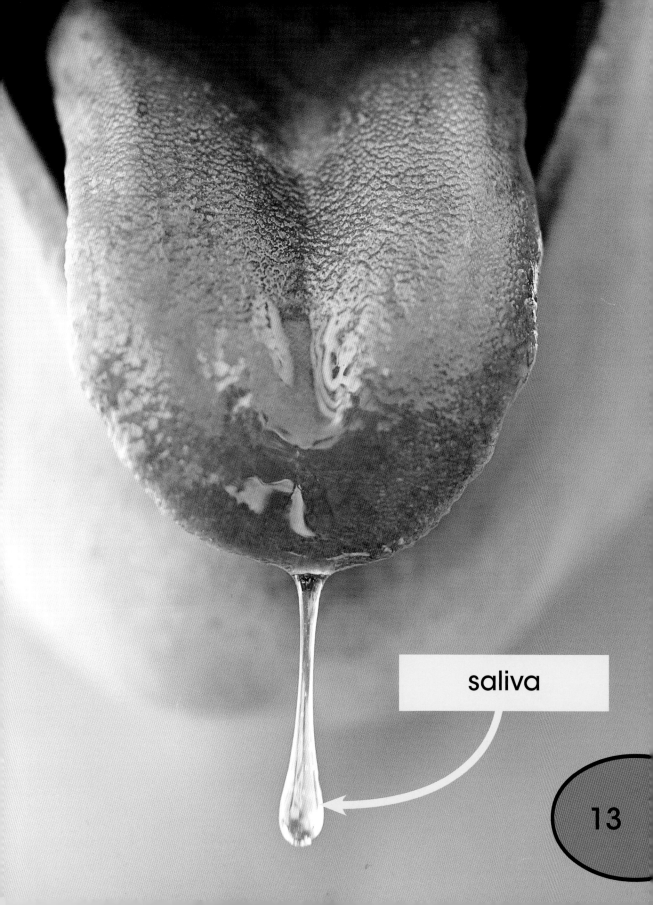

saliva

13

Ear wax

Ear wax keeps your ears clean! Wax slowly makes its way out of your ears. Any dirt comes out with it. Sometimes the wax sticks together to make an orange-yellow lump.

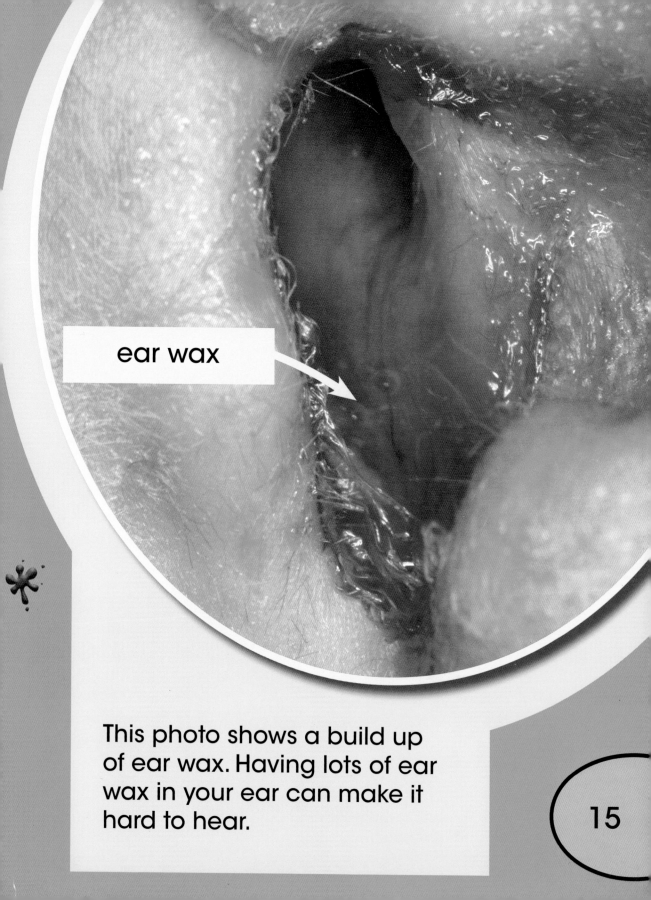

ear wax

This photo shows a build up of ear wax. Having lots of ear wax in your ear can make it hard to hear.

Conjunctivitis

Conjunctivitis gives you sticky goo on your eyelids. The goo makes it hard to open your eyes in the morning. Conjunctivitis is also called pink eye. It is caused by a type of **germ** called **bacteria**.

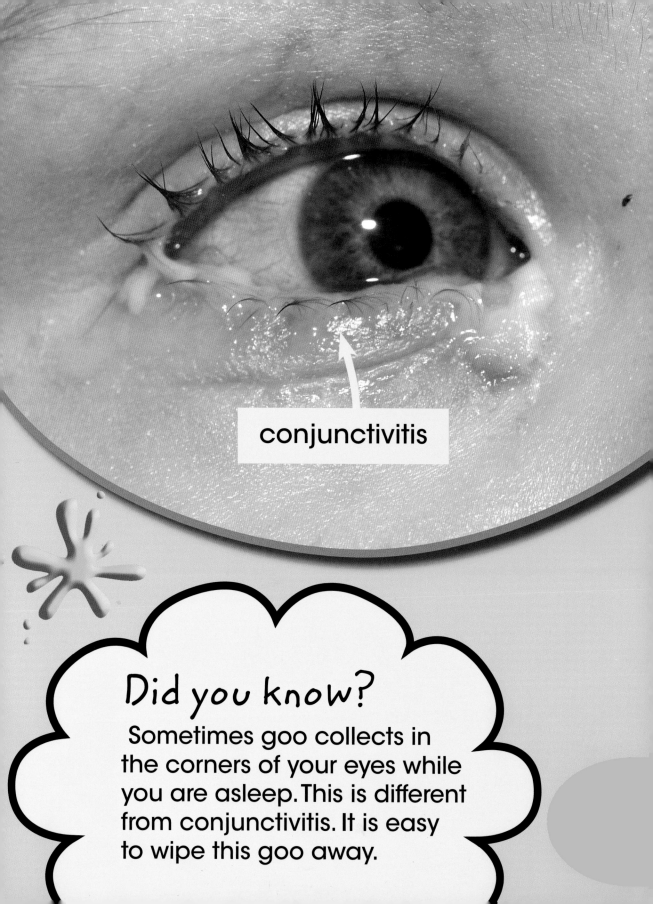

conjunctivitis

Did you know?
Sometimes goo collects in the corners of your eyes while you are asleep. This is different from conjunctivitis. It is easy to wipe this goo away.

Bleeding

If you scratch or make a small cut to your skin, blood oozes out. Don't panic! Bleeding washes out dirt and **germs.** You still need to clean the cut under running water, and cover it with a sticking plaster.

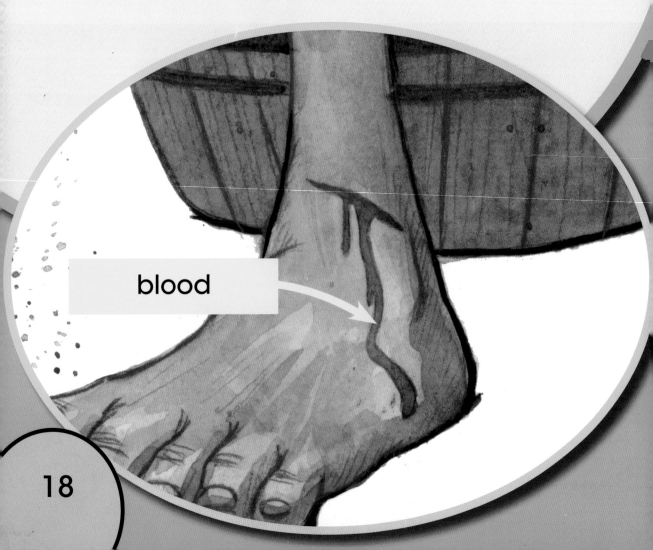

blood

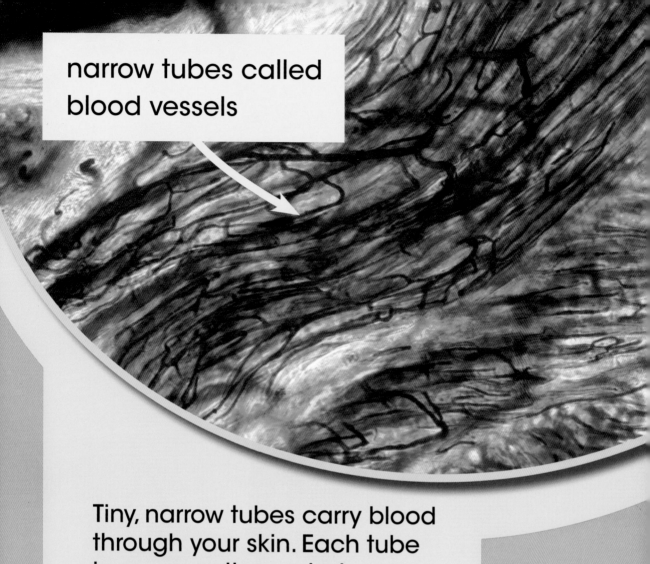

narrow tubes called
blood vessels

Tiny, narrow tubes carry blood
through your skin. Each tube
is narrower than a hair on
your head.

WARNING
If you cut yourself find
someone to help you.

19

Scabs

A small cut will soon stop bleeding. This is because the blood in the cut becomes thicker. It forms a thick blob. This thick blob slowly dries to form a hard scab.

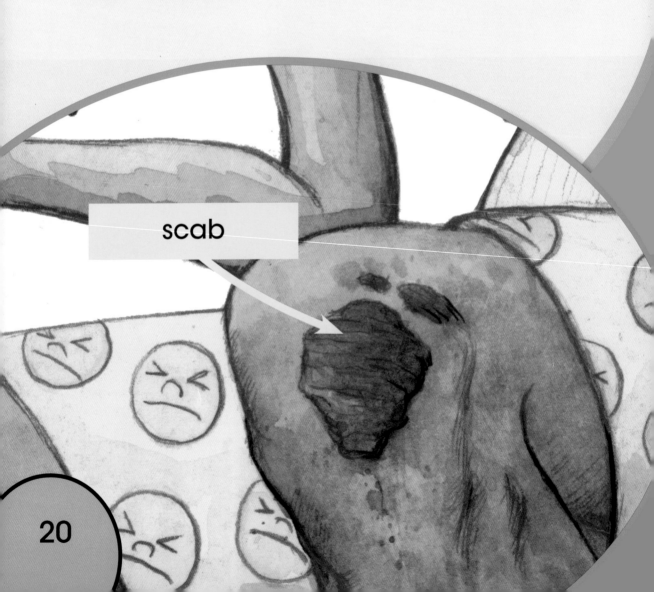

scab

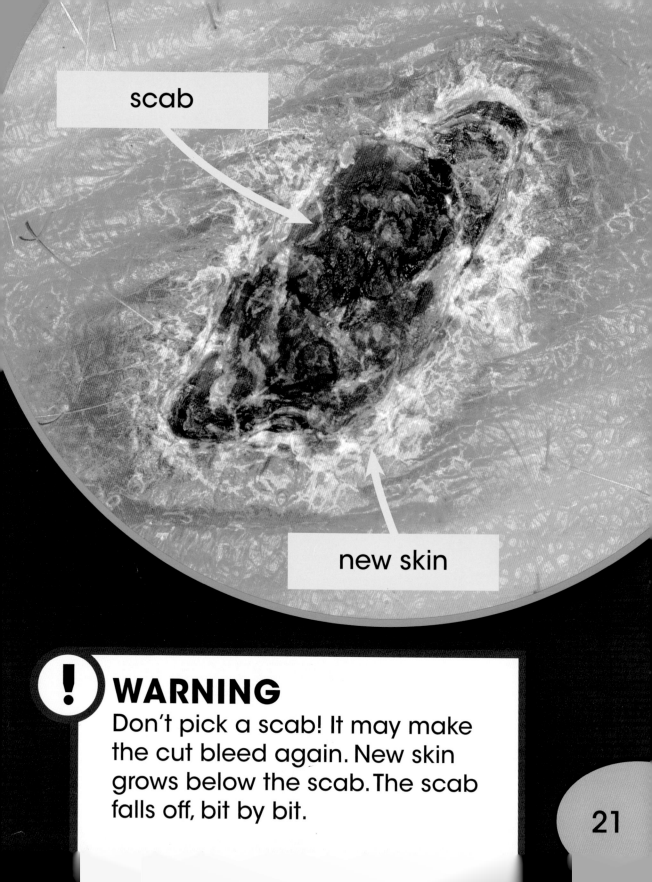

scab

new skin

⊘ WARNING

Don't pick a scab! It may make the cut bleed again. New skin grows below the scab. The scab falls off, bit by bit.

Boils

A boil is a spot that is filled with **pus**. If the boil bursts, the pus oozes out. Pus is a thick liquid. It contains **germs** from inside the spot.

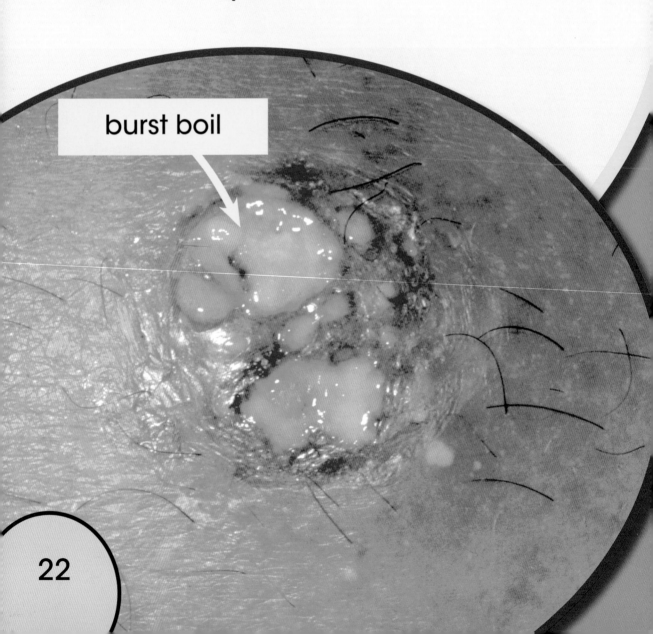

burst boil

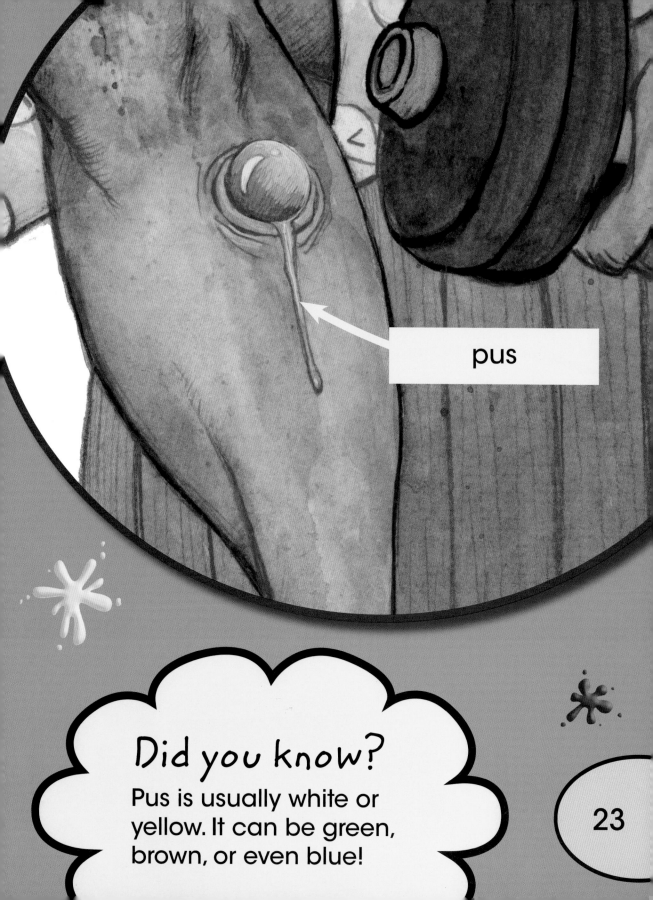

pus

Did you know?
Pus is usually white or yellow. It can be green, brown, or even blue!

Sweat

Sweat is liquid that oozes out of your skin. Sweat helps to keep you cool. The hotter you are the more you sweat. Old sweat may become smelly.

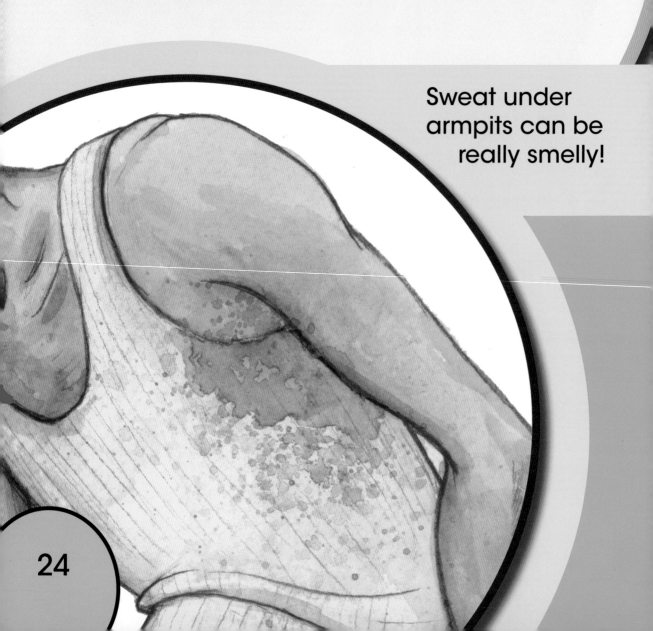

Sweat under armpits can be really smelly!

24

Did you know?

Running around makes you sweat even more. Footballers can lose 9 litres of sweat a day. That's the same as about 36 glasses of water.

Smelly feet

Your feet sweat. They sweat even more when you wear trainers. Old sweat in your trainers makes your trainers stink too.

More about body fluids

More than half of your body is water.

Blood and wee are mostly water. So are **saliva**, **mucus**, snot, and tears.

You lose more than a litre of water every day. You lose most of it in wee, sweat, poo, and in the air you breathe out.

You should drink about 1 to 2 litres of liquid a day. This will help to replace the water you lose.

You make about 1 to 2 litres of saliva every day.

1 to 2 litres is about 4 to 8 glasses.

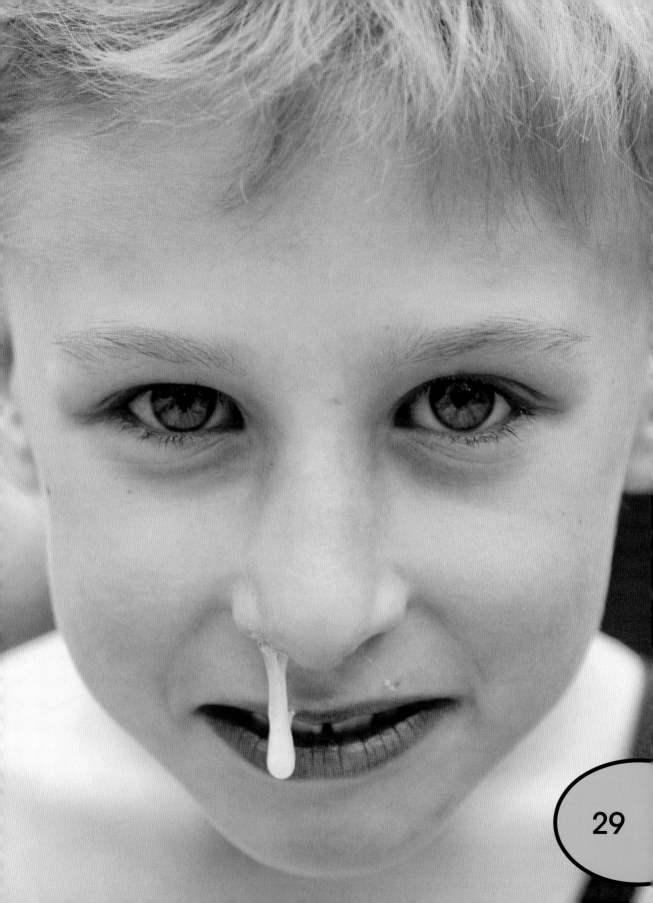

Glossary

bacteria tiny living things. Bacteria are a type of germ.

conjunctivitis an illness that affects the inside of the eyelid

ear wax soft, yellow wax that is made by the skin in the ear

germs tiny living things that can make you ill if they get inside your body

lungs parts of your body where air goes when you breathe in. You have two lungs in your chest.

mucus slimy liquid that lines the tubes inside your body

phlegm mucus made in your breathing tubes

pus a thick yellow or white liquid that forms when a cut is infected by germs

saliva liquid made in the mouths of people, insects, and other kinds of animals. Saliva is also called "spit".

Find out more

Find out

Do animals get snotty noses too?

Books

How's Your Health? Colds and Flu,
Angela Royston (Franklin Watts, 2006)

My Best Book of the Human Body, Barbara Taylor
(Kingfisher Books, 2008)

Up Close Human Body, Paul Harrison
(Franklin Watts, 2009)

Websites

**kids.aol.co.uk/slimey-facts-about-snot/
article/20080707101809990001**
This fun website is full of interesting facts about
mucus or snot.

kidshealth.org/kid/ill_injure/sick/colds.html
This website tells you about colds and mucus. It
also explains how your body fights germs.

**www.childrenfirst.nhs.uk/kids/health/illnesses/
c/colds.html**
This website tells you about colds and how you
catch them.

Index